MEN ARE FROM MARS... I'M FROM NORWICH

By Roger McCartney

MEN ARE FROM MARS
I'M FROM
NORWICH

<u>Copyright</u>

ISBN:
9781521768501

Imprint:
Independently
published

BY ROGER MCCARTNEY 2

<u>Introduction</u>

Narrrwich women, prepare to be enlightened. Norwich men prepare to be compromised!

You will laugh as you read all about Canary male behaviour, and the Wensum-side perspective on life. The book is chocka with humourous observations and man-secrets.

This book is a celebration of all things NR; the people, the city and the language. It's bootiful bor. It's not about the author being from

MEN ARE FROM MARS
I'M FROM
NORWICH

Norwich, it's about the reader being from Norwich.

BY ROGER MCCARTNEY 4

MEN ARE FROM MARS
I'M FROM
NORWICH

Contents

BY ROGER MCCARTNEY 5

MEN ARE FROM MARS
I'M FROM
NORWICH

BY ROGER MCCARTNEY 6

<u>*Man Secret #1*</u>: Norwich Man is The King of Procrastination

Procrastination is a concept already familiar down at Carra Rud; we'll win the Champions League next season, thank you very much.

But it suddenly hit me the other day when I was walking down Earlham Road, and I don't mean the tree outside the Co-op. It was the following thought that hit me: all my life, I have been dogged by procrastination. And I'm going to tell you exactly why this is bor, some other time.

Indeed, whilst writing this celebration of the Canary mind-set, I am putting off several other things that I should have already done by now. And Norwich City Football Club too are putting a few things off, like the acquisition of points,

BY ROGER MCCARTNEY 7

because we should be a lot higher up the Championship than we presently are.

Yellows men have a saying: "we'll get the three points *next week*". I don't know where this saying came from. Probably from ancient times. Alan Irvine, maybe. He's ancient. I'll have to google it later. Never do anything today that you can put off until tomorrow.

Canary women are adept at doing several tasks at once. This is called **multitasking**. I read about that in the *Eastern Daily Press*. Norwich men, however, are equally as adept at *putting off* several tasks at once. This is known as '**multi-thinking-about-but-not-actually-doing-any-tasking**.'

We will routinely postpone everything until the middle of next week, and then postpone it further if there is a midweek match. My **laundry** will be done only when we spot our socks making their own way over to the washing machine. **Bills**

BY ROGER MCCARTNEY 8

will only get paid when the bailiff personally presents them.

My **car** will only be washed once people are starting to write childish messages, with their fingers in the dirt - such as "up the canaries" and "I wish my wife was as dirty as this". Ok, admittedly, I write the messages on the car myself, sometimes!

Health is the easiest issue to procrastinate over. You know when you get an appointment at the Norfolk and Norwich for six months or even a year's time – that suits me! Shink I'm proper head in the sand, me. I do so hate to receive bad news of a medical nature, I do. Ruins the day. I much prefer to schedule an endoscopy for next year. And then in the Close Season or at worst, an international break.

If the problem is anything to do with 'downstairs', then you can forget it altogether. Funny that – men from Norwich love to wave their genitals about on a boozy night out down

MEN ARE FROM MARS
I'M FROM
NORWICH

the Fat Cap Brewery Tap but ask them for a medical examination of said genitals and they disappear for longer than Gazza, in-between benders.

Our ladies, on the other hand, love a visit to the doctors, they do. I think the fact that the male locums look like George Clooney may have something to do with her real motivation to visit with such regularity, do you know what I mean? She indoors will make an appointment just to discuss colour co-ordination schemes in the lounge or to announce a new apple crumble recipe she is planning.

The reason for Norwich male procrastination is simple. We are primarily hunter/gatherers. In-between hunting and gathering expeditions, we maximise our downtime. Cavemen used to loaf about the cave. We like to loaf about in front of *Goals on Sunday* with Ben and Kammy.

BY ROGER MCCARTNEY 10

After a hard day's hunting and gathering all day, we like to come home to our caves and be nurtured by our favourite Norwich cavewoman. It's been that way since old Mother Matthew's little boy, Bernard, coined the phrase 'bootiful'. Cawd da hell bor. New age Norwich man? I'm only just catching up with pre-Tescos Extra in Sprowston, Norwich-man!

One or two things have changed in the last two million years though. Shink so. The Perseverance on Adelaide Street has closed and Carra Rud has been revamped. Women now work, and men occasionally look after babies. Can you imagine a stay-at-home cave husband back in ancient times looking after the juniors while the *woman* went out and slaughtered a mammoth? It Didn't happen, bor.

Narrrwich Man should not be castigated for his procrastinating nature though. It takes stern resolution and serious prioritisation skills - for us to balance a busy life at home and work and

pub - and still be able to fit in eight hours watching Sky Sports.

God willing and more importantly, partner willing, there will still be five minutes left at the end of the day, after *Match of the Day*, in which to get cosy with the missus. This is one appointment we do not wish to defer to a later date!

That is, if your partner hasn't sulked off because you procrastinate so much. Or maybe she's a procrastinator too and keeps *putting off* sulking off until another day.

But hold yew hard. A girlfriend of mine used to say; "You'll never amount to anything because you procrastinate too much, you do." I used to say, **"leave it out, slow yew down, let's just wait and see!"**

BY ROGER MCCARTNEY 12

Man Secret #2: It's a Myth That Norwich Men Think About Sex Every Six Sec...

There is a body of experts out by there, who, we shall for the purposes of this discussion, label 'Norwich women' - that think that another body of people – whom we shall loosely call 'Norwich men' – think about sex with about the regularity of every six seconds.

The six-second premise was first put forward by someone, probably a female, a very long time ago, in order to explain why us men, have the morality code of the lesser-spotted porcupine.

The six-second gambit is an oft-quoted falsehood about the male of the Norwich

BY ROGER MCCARTNEY 13

species. This myth, together with 'all men from the greater Norwich area are naturally gifted at DIY', is often wide of the mark.

There are other myths perpetuated about Norwich men; for example, that they all are obsessed with Norwich City Football Club. They are not: some men are obsessed with that other great team in the world: Norwich City Football Club reserves. Another myth is that all men talk about when they get with other men is football. They don't: they talk about women...that talk about football; although admittedly in between breaks from talking about football.

Of course, in reality, the idea that an Narrrwich man thinks saucy thoughts twice during the time it takes Wayne Rooney to take a corner for England, is quite frankly, absurd. Preposterous! Do you not know anything about men? It's a lot more frequent than that, bor.

BY ROGER MCCARTNEY 14

Yep, the male of the species is much dirtier than the female. We all know that, we do. Sexual thoughts are omni-present. Why? Because we are men. That is what we do. That is what we are best at, is it? Sexual thoughts are like Cameron Jerome goals - you don't have one for ages and then you get one and after that they don't stop coming.

Our brains are like call centres; "The next sexual image will be arriving in your mind just now, in a minute, is it? Please hold – your continued interest is important to us"

Of course, we think about women every six seconds. It would be impossible not to. But don't be too down on us; we also think about next week's match every four seconds as well like. In the time it takes Usain Bolt to murder the opposition, we have thought about sex three times and we're pondering next week's tricky away trip to Middlesbrough?

BY ROGER MCCARTNEY 15

MEN ARE FROM MARS
I'M FROM
NORWICH

Do not give us any grief about it though. Have pity on us for we know not what we do, is it? We cannot help it. We're men, bor. Let she who is without sin throw the first stone.

Ouch, watch where you are throwing those stones, will you! You had berra pack that in gel!

BY ROGER MCCARTNEY 16

Man Secret #3: Norwich Men Don't Do Platonic.

I had a woman as a friend once. I know, tidy as you like. We used to work together and meet up at the Belgian Monk at lunch time for a bite to eat. Our common ground was a mutual interest in getting mildly drunk in the lunch break. And I so wanted to sleep with her.

Which brings me to the Deal or No Deal question and I'm ready to be asked it. Can a Norwich guy have a friendship with a Norwich girl, without wanting to sleep with her?

The short answer is no. The longer answer may lead me to further compromise the Norwich brotherhood, by revealing yet more official man-secrets.

So, buckle up, and enjoy the ride!

BY ROGER MCCARTNEY 17

Anyone, who knows the Norwich masculine mind-set – in other words; men from Norwich - will tell you that we *don't do* platonic. We would like to but we can't. We haven't got it in us. End of.

What we do have in us - is a massive amount of raging testosterone and a burning desire to finish above Ipswich. Oh, and did I mention a primeval desire to mate with every female on the planet? Even those from Catton Grove. Admittedly, the passing of time and the advent of kebab-induced obesity have tempered this prehistoric urge, but it is still in the mix somewhere. We keep it hidden, but in our minds - everyone is being assessed as a potential sleeping partner. We can't help this thought process.

There are no female friends; just lovers waiting to happen. Norwich men, if they're truthful, will agree with this philosophy. If they *don't* admit to it, they may tend to haemorrhage credibility.

BY ROGER MCCARTNEY 18

Norwich women unwittingly put themselves in the frontline, by liking us 'as a friend'. Expect the male side of the partnership to be looking to upgrade his 'friend' status, anytime soon. Friendships with the opposite sex are love affairs in the early stages – hopefully.

Back to the Belgian Monk ladette: She never knew of my aspirations to date her and I certainly never let on, for her boyfriend was a bang tidy six-foot ten rugby player from Aylsham. She was fascinated with me for my ability to consume three lunchtime pints, and I was fascinated by her - for her very existence. I used to look longingly into her hazel eyes and lust after her ruby lips as she chomped on her bacon & egg sarnie. She, in return, looked imploringly at me, for another white wine spritzer.

She used to bring her friend along sometimes by here, and I so fancied her as well. In fact, come to think of it, I so fancied everyone that came along. I've had many female friends over the

BY ROGER MCCARTNEY 19

years, and I've wanted to sleep with all of them. Sometimes, male ego being what it is, I'll think I've met *The One* if a woman lets me out on St Crispins Road.

Female companions are always better than same-sex ones because the possibility exists of sleeping with them. With a fellow man, you just don't have that option available to you. No, it's all about bonding over pints, and conversation that alternates between Messi's ability and Beyoncé's bottom. All very riveting, but it doesn't pay the bills and it don't satisfy the inherent latent primeval cravings. **Give me Miss Ruby Lips up the Belgian and her bacon & egg sarnie prop any day.**

Man Secret #4: What Wensum-side Fellas Really Think About Rotund Norwich Women.

This week I have been besieged by Norwich-based females demanding to know what Norwich men **really** think of their partners, being a touch rotund. Well, one woman from Plumstead Road has politely asked, so here goes.

Of course, I could give you a truthful account but as it goes against the man-code to reveal our secrets – if I told you, then I would have to kill you. However, in the interests of the book, here is the absolute truth, even if my instincts are to say nothing and scratch my genitals.

To get a quiet life with the minimum amount of chew like, Norwich men have developed a knee-jerk reaction under questioning about weight

BY ROGER MCCARTNEY 21

issues. If we value having a full set of testicles – which we do – and to prevent our women kicking off ba, we will automatically respond in the negative when asked questions such as "does my bum look big in this?" Answer anything other than negative and there's going to be hell on.

Here's the rub. I am **not** lying, **I am telling the truth, I am.** If I thought my woman was not fanciable, I wouldn't fancy her. Ergo, I wouldn't be with her. Or more importantly - I wouldn't have got with her in the first place. What more conclusive proof do you need of my sincerity during ~~interrogation~~ questioning?

Sure, we would all like to have girlfriends that look like Kim Kardashian. That is a given. In fact, we would all like to have for a girlfriend, Kim Kardashian, but this is just not possible. Just as Santa cannot get around every house in Norwich, neither can Kim.

Besides, this is real world, UK, and just as us Norwich men don't look like David de Gea - the

MEN ARE FROM MARS
I'M FROM
NORWICH

ones that do are keepers, aren't they? – Norwich women don't look like Kim Kardashian. Not round our way in Earlham Road, anyway. And if the women in our street did look like her, I would probably be too shy to go up and talk to them. Real women have love handles. Accept the fact. Deal with it. Move on.

I don't expect my women to be perfect in much the same way, as I'm not. My waistline is like the Larkman on a Saturday night – it needs continual policing. I also have a boil on my bottom, but we don't need to go there. Real women are no less desirable than their airbrushed counterparts – and, they have the elusive quality that Kim does not – they are attainable.

During my observations, several of my acquaintances have gone on about being over-weight, when there was absolutely nowt wrong with them. Trips to Sportspark and splodging about at Yarmouth have had to be aborted or she will turn up looking like Lawrence of Arabia.

BY ROGER MCCARTNEY 23

Sometimes women will even request, "Don't look at me bor!" when they take their clothes off. Well how is that going to work then? Am I supposed to move in for a spot of lovemaking by using the handy Braille signposting provided?

It seems to me that Narrrwich women feel they have to attain stick insect like qualities. You are joking, bor. These women look positively underfed. I want to take them home not to have my wicked way but to give them some a decent meal. Under-nourishment is not an attractive quality; you know?

I am not going to lie to you and say that I find obesity attractive. I personally don't although some Norwich men do. There is a line, you know. However, curves attract us Canary men. Simple as. **We are programmed to fancy you,** rounded tummy or not. I must be honest and say that the law of diminishing returns will occur after the acceptable level of curviness has been reached - and that's the science out of the way - but this

BY ROGER MCCARTNEY 24

MEN ARE FROM MARS
I'M FROM
NORWICH

level is **way beyond what most Norwich women
would think. Shink so!**

BY ROGER MCCARTNEY 25

Man Secret #5: Norwich Man Is Rubbish at DIY. Fact.

It's a fact of life, that men from Norwich are expected to be naturals at DIY. We are the men not from Del Monte but from Mousehold, so get on and fix it bor!

As soon as something goes pear-shaped, or the downstairs toilet pipes begin crying out to have a nice little timber unit fashioned around them, then the man will become firmly fixed in the gaze of expectation. In my experience, this is one of the downsides to having the XY chromosomes.

What it is, even though Norwich history was fashioned by men from the coal industry, we are not all industrious here on the Wensum. In fact, some of us are craftsmanship-challenged but

BY ROGER MCCARTNEY 26

then the table from IKEA I've just assembled, cack-handedly, back-to-front, kind of gives it away, like.

Of course, our women could and should call in the experts, but to allow this would be an admission of failure as a man. The very thought of another fella coming in to do a job when we have enough limbs and fingers, would be the DIY equivalent of being cuckolded.

The reasons for this expectation of Norwich men lie in our caveman roots, when DIY was first invented to ensure survival of the fittest. We sat in our caves, is it, fashioning crude objects out of wood and stone, while the woman prepared roast mammoth for lunch.

Two million years later and things have progressed. Rather than worship the moon, we now can play golf on it. However, I am still sat here attempting to fashion crude objects out of wood and stone.

BY ROGER MCCARTNEY 27

Modern day DIY is primarily to ensure the amusement of the fattest. Success at it feeds directly into our self-esteem and, more importantly; feeds directly into the esteem our women have for us. Our qualities as the provider may be under examination. The provider of shelving units, which do not slope, that is.

At school at the Hewett Academy, I just didn't get woodwork and metalwork. Sure, I was inventive with excuses, but I wasn't so resourceful when it Came to shaping the materials into anything remotely discernible. No wonder I used to skive off home to watch afternoon telly. I didn't foresee that one day my life's purpose would come down to the alignment of two holes in the wall. I also didn't foresee the Headmaster would tan my backside for skiving. But that's another story.

Because I never listened at school and haven't since been to University to get a degree in engineering, my aptitude for DIY is severely

BY ROGER MCCARTNEY 28

restricted and has cursed me all my life. I was 32 before I owned a screwdriver and I was 35 before I used it. My toolbox was stolen once, and I was secretly relieved. The Missus kept quiet because she needed someone to assemble the thirty-two flat packs she just ordered from MFI.

The only thing that *will* come naturally to me when things start to go wrong will be the expletives. I will swear and cuss like that lad Teesside Tintin. Call it up on *You Tube*, if you're not familiar. That lad will have nothing on me like, once I've nailed my hand to the table a few times. Indeed, I will be a lot more inventive in the creation of profanities than in the creation of furniture, is it?

I will become so irritated, after stabbing my thumb for the third time, that I'll destroy the very object I am trying to construct. This defeats the purpose of DIY, which is to build things, not to demolish them, halfway through the process, once you have part-crucified

yourself. And when I drop the hammer on my toe, I will dance and shriek like, with more dexterity than that lad Michael Jackson. Then we'll see who's bad!

I suppose my ineptitude could be hereditary as I remember that in my childhood back when men were men and sheep were scared, our dad always used to saw into the table and electrocute himself routinely. He used to get proper agitated too. When they were giving brains out, he thought they said 'trains' and he asked for a slow one. Was he daft? A little I suppose; he married mother, is it?

On Completion of tasks, I will expect much praise and promises of cuddling, later from her like. Otherwise the next time she asks me to put a picture up I might just answer in the true spirit of DIY and say, **"Do it yourself, bor!"**

BY ROGER MCCARTNEY 30

Man Secret #6: Norwich Man Has Difficulty Saying, 'I Love You'.

Norwich men are not very emotional. Apparently. Apart from when Norwich lose in the playoffs or get relegated. Then we are emotional.

This allegation of our un-emotional-ness arises from our reluctance to say the sentence that can mean so much to a woman - and it is not **'Shall I empty the bin, gel?'**

No, the group of words that causes us the greatest consternation and the one I personally have difficulty marshalling to my lips is **'I love you'**.

A Norwich man will enthuse "I **love** the _Murderers_- best pub in Norwich'. But ask him to

BY ROGER MCCARTNEY 31

use 'love' in a statement of endearment towards his life-partner and *it becomes a different matter,* as the man in the Heineken ad used to say.

'Sorry' is a word that is easy to say. I will spray 'sorry' around liberally, all day if necessary. Each time I bump into someone – 'sorry'. Each time I tread on someone's toes – 'sorry'. Each time she says, 'You really hurt me, you' – 'sorry'.

'Sorry' is the catch-all remedy that makes everything better. It is instant verbal healing. "Sorry, we threw away a two-goal lead". In football, when the trainer applies the magic spray to the injured player's leg – that is the aerosol form of 'sorry'.

Just as I reserve the wearing of my Wales Rugby shirt for Sunday best, I will keep back the phrase **'I love you'** for special occasions too, I will.

BY ROGER MCCARTNEY 32

I will only say it when I am backed into a corner and a proclamation of fondness is the only way out. In partnership-threatening situations, such as an argument, the statement can save the day. If utilised correctly, it can be the injection of adrenaline that an ailing or stagnant relationship needs.

Sometimes, I will use the **'love you'** card tactically, like, to get what I want is it, smooth things over or to put points in the affection bank.

Besides, relationship protocol demands you must sprinkle the phrase into the mix occasionally, otherwise your boyfriend skills may be deemed to suck. If you are not careful you are then heading for the resultant **'you never say you love me'** discussion – and no one wants to go down that road. That may lead on to 'you never express yourself, you'. At this point, I will be fighting hard the urge to express myself by throttling her.

BY ROGER MCCARTNEY 33

So why are the three words of adoration, so difficult? Firstly, '**I love you**', is coming from a place deep down in your heart. By reaching down to find this sentiment, you are opening a duct directly into your soul. Good stuff such as '**I love you**' can come out, but equally bad stuff, such as '**I hate you**' can get in. Best to keep the entrance to this channel always blocked by triviality .

Secondly, '**I love you**' is an admission of weakness. It goes against the manly grain. I may as well say 'Please walk all over me – and don't forget to lock up, afterwards!'

As a man, I must be tough, not weak, is it. It's part of the skillset. I don't do weakness, me. Weakness is not going to protect against the sabre-toothed tiger when it comes bounding into the cave or nowadays, when the burglar comes creeping into the house, late at night. Perhaps I

BY ROGER MCCARTNEY 34

can persuade him to put the metal piping down by telling him I love *him*?

The next time your man has fallen short of the regulation thirty expressions of devotion per month, don't berate him - treat him kindly. He's an emotionally stunted cripple for good reason, do you know what I mean mun?

Here's an idea: tell him that *you* love him, like, for as far as the 'I love you' declaration goes – **I think it's far nicer to receive than it is to give. Shud think so.**

BY ROGER MCCARTNEY 35

Man Secret #7: Norwich Men Hate Shopping.

I'm not being funny but the next relationship I get into; I'm going to find out from the outset if we're shopping-soul mates.

Apart from needing to know if we are suited in the bedroom department, I need to know if we are suited in the department-store department.

If we are going to be spending a good proportion of 'us time' in intu Chapelfield, particularly in the acquisition of new clothes *for her*, it makes sense to find out if we're intu-chapelfield-compatible? The couple that shops together stays together. Although this is not strictly true as she will no doubt keep mooching off.

My preference is for the SAS style of shopping - get in, get the purchase and get out again in as quick a time as possible. This renders me

BY ROGER MCCARTNEY 36

practically useless as good female company. If I could I would even hoy in a stun grenade to facilitate the encounter. Ideally, I would be so quick that even the CCTV would not pick me up by here, which is good, as then I can't be prosecuted for the grenade-throwing incident.

Of course, the missus will out-shop me every time, she will. Even when we are in B & Q, looking at power-saws, she is enjoying the experience more than I am.

The only time I genuinely enjoy shopping is when we are in Tesco Norwich, food shopping. It says on the job-specification of a man that he is the number one provider – so there is a certain amount of role fulfilment to be had for the man, in the attainment of the weekly provisions.

I find clothes shopping a far more irksome task. It is a lot quicker and easier watching grass grow - and at least you get to sit down a bit. I don't like anything, apart from German Village and Bierfest, which lasts half a day or more.

BY ROGER MCCARTNEY 37

She is far better to go shopping with Captain Canary, the Norwich FC mascot or someone, anyone, other than me.

My standing-up span is severely limited, and I will immediately collapse, upon entering a shop, into the nearest chair. You will usually find me in the footwear department not checking out the loafers – but instead - loafing on the chairs provided, watching *Final Score*, if possible.

Buying clothes is like decorating the lounge: it's decoration of the human torso. Embellishment is best left to the female. Just as I wouldn't contest her selection of sequinned cushions, from Norwich market, I also wouldn't interfere in her choice of frock.

After she's spent an hour trying them all on in *New Look* she will breeze out of the shop, saying that nothing suited. I am not so foolish to think that we won't be back before the day is out to pick up the outfit that she secretly liked is it?

BY ROGER MCCARTNEY 38

The amount of time I have spent waiting outside changing rooms. You don't get that time back butt. And if you did get it back, God with his sense of irony would probably allocate you a few more hours in *Dorothy Perkins* or something.

Canary women are at home in clothing outlets. Simple as. I suspect they all have that inner catwalk model in them trying to get out, even if the audience consists of only a disgruntled partner and a mirror.

The upside for me is that I get to see her in various stages of dress and undress. And as an unexpected bonus I may get to see other women in various stages of dress and undress as I hang around the changing rooms - legitimately this time.

And if I grunt enough encouraging approvals, I might get treated to the treasured *Quarter Pounder* afterwards. I'm absolutely gasping for a *Mcdonalds* after me shopping trip like.

BY ROGER MCCARTNEY 39

MEN ARE FROM MARS
I'M FROM
NORWICH

Forget Chapelfield. A burger topped with cheese. Bootiful! **Now that's my type of shopping!**

BY ROGER MCCARTNEY 40

MEN ARE FROM MARS
I'M FROM
NORWICH

Man Secret #8: Norwich Women That Norwich Men Like to Avoid

As a card-carrying, red-blooded Norwich fella, I like to meet women across a wide spectrum of different types and women. Providing they are carrying the necessary double x chromosomal pattern then they're in. Simple as. However, there is one type of woman that I like to give a wide berth to, when assessing potential partners. These are, of course, Norwich women that delight in copying the behaviour of Norwich men: **Ladettes**. Nightmare. I proper like to avoid them, I do.

Ladettes are often more laddish than the lads they are trying to replicate. Only one problem: we don't like it. If we wanted a female companion to be a lad, we would just simply place an ad for a lad. Once women start acting

BY ROGER MCCARTNEY 41

masculine, they neutralise their sexuality, which in turn neutralises their attractiveness. The whole attraction of women to us is built upon the assumption that they are just that, WOMEN. Once the lines of gender become blurred you might just as well have a game of snooker with her indoors and go to bed with Graham Souness.

Ladettes alarm us because they out-male us. They play football. They like to drink pints, laugh raucously and stub out cigarettes on our hands. They are often better fighters than we are and, can out drink us. What's the point in having one for a girlfriend? I'm not having it like. It's like having a date with Joey Barton.

In the bedroom, they also try to out-do us by being more macho and throwing us around the room a little. And that's just the foreplay! Now that's not on! We men like to be in charge in the bedroom or at very least be kept informed as to what's happening. I once knew a woman that turned out to be this type. I met her in the *Fat*

Cat, and she had fists, just like a couple of fat cats as well. If I'd known what our night of wrestling was going to be like I would have asked her to go gentle with me, as it was my first time with a sexually aggressive woman, me. And last. Hopefully.

In the bedroom, well, it all kicked off in there didn't it? She proceeded to bounce us off the walls and tug us in places I didn't even know were official tugging zones, like. She was asking all the questions like, but I didn't have any of the answers. It was shocking. The next morning, I enquired if she knew the whereabouts of my testicles. On receiving her answer, I collected them from the far-flung corners of the room and fled. I swear by here, down on my mum's life, never again bor.

Anno, it was awful. I was lucky to escape with my life, not to mention my testicles. I am still not sure if she qualified as a ladette or just an out and out nutter. And as I have been proven

BY ROGER MCCARTNEY 43

to be a nutter-magnet, I suppose it could be the latter.

Read my lips: We men don't like women to be more sexually voracious than we are. Voracity is our job. Comes with the turf. We are the Norwich men. Canaries on our shirts. Call me old-school, but we men will do all the necessary bouncing and tugging, thank you very much! Over-zealousness on the part of the female is guaranteed to kill 99% of all household erections. If I wanted that sort of interaction with a female, I would enter the Hellesdon mixed sumo-wrestling championships.

In my view, women are supposed to act demurely and flutter their eyelids as they blush at the very mention of the bedroom. Not turn into Ricky Savage on a bad hair day, the moment the bedroom door is locked. That scares me as it would do any red-blooded male and then the only woman, **I want then is my mum.**

BY ROGER MCCARTNEY 44

Man Secret #9: What, Apart from Relegation, Makes Norwich Men Cry?

I didn't do sensitivity until I was twenty-one, me. That was the day the golden-haired girl from around the corner in Gladstone Street decided it was over. Then I became sensitive.

Growing up, I had always adhered to the 'big boys don't cry' rule. You were not allowed to cry except when Norwich got relegated - so quite often then. But from the age of five I was expected to be striving towards manhood, and not bawling like a baby. By adulthood, I was an automaton, devoid of feeling altogether. If I so much as showed a nano-second of emotion, amid my peer group, I would receive the punishment of being jeered to death.

BY ROGER MCCARTNEY 45

But this new adult pain, initiated by the honey-haired one, was altogether different. The sadness was so great, that the emotion had nowhere else to go other than to explode out through my tear ducts. And I didn't give a monkey's what the peer group thought.

She was the person who first tweaked my crying nerve. In our short time together, we shared a crash course in love. When our love inevitably *did* crash, the lesson became 'how to cry', for she had given me good reason to. The mourning period for that relationship lasted longer than the relationship itself. Kleenex was looking to sponsor me, and my mates were looking to give me a good kicking, if I didn't shape up. "are yew coming to see the Canaries, bor. She's only a gel!" they said.

"You wait, yew see," I snivelled, and sure enough, one by one, they were all struck down by the heartbreak-virus. It was my turn to gloat

and provide the anti-virus – alcohol - and profound slogans – among them "she's only a gel!"

Professional counselling could have helped us, but I embarked on a more immediate remedy – drinking myself silly. Drink only made things worse, and then I really *did* need counselling – for alcohol addiction. I used to ring AA so regularly, the guy, who was getting pulled out of the the Wig and Pen each time to come on the phone, was getting proper agitated.

My decline into soft-heartedness accelerated as I got older and I have now even been reduced to crying now when *we score a goal* instead of the more traditional tear-inducing conceding of a goal, as you would expect. It's a happy form of crying like, although to protect the man-status I need to sob as inconspicuously as possible. I will deliver each droplet down my cheek as quietly as possible me like. I was not expecting to sob for England when I sat down this

BY ROGER MCCARTNEY 47

MEN ARE FROM MARS
I'M FROM
NORWICH

afternoon in front of the tele for Norwich's latest outing.

Although the letting down of the manly guard is regrettable, I find that sobbing in front of a woman can be beneficial too. It may result in much female nurturing and soothing. As a young'un, a gashed knee would result in the immediate requirement for mother. Now, I run to the missus, retaining as much macho poise as possible even if tears are streaming.

This interaction is like saying to her, "You take over the reins for a moment whilst I have this mini-breakdown like, and then we'll resume as normal." She may be pleased she's chosen a compassionate human being for a companion – or riled that she's chosen a cry-baby. Failing that, and I'm on the phone to mum.

I don't know why I cry. Maybe it was Norwich failing dismally one too many times. Maybe I'm a bit of a miserable get with 'unhappy' stamped on my soul, or maybe I still miss Goldilocks. She

BY ROGER MCCARTNEY 48

was the one that released the dam that had been waiting to burst; all those years of stubbing my toe, having my virility questioned in the changing rooms, and Norwich getting knocked out early doors. That was a huge back-catalogue of tears! We Norwich men are only human. If you cut us, do we not bleed yellow and green? **And we are likely to cry as well.**

MEN ARE FROM MARS
I'M FROM
NORWICH

Man Secret #10:
Question: Do Norwich Men Cheat? Answer: Is Delia Smith a Cook?

I tell you what it is: the good news is that not all Norwich men cheat. Here on the Wensum we are made of stern stuff. We are a manufacturing town but, we are not in the market of manufacturing cheating and neither do we all have the testicular fortitude. These 'thoroughly nice Norwich blokes' make ideal husband material and are known as 'keepers' as basically there is no reason to boot them out.

The bad news is that the rest of the Norwich male population are actively cheating, thinking of cheating or would cheat if an opportunity comes along. The Norwich brotherhood will deny

BY ROGER MCCARTNEY 50

MEN ARE FROM MARS
I'M FROM
NORWICH

it, but then we claim the right to remain silent in case we incriminate ourselves.

I personally am between cheats now, as you need a primary relationship in order to cheat on it with a secondary one.

So why do Norwich men cheat? I'm not going to tell you that it lies in our evolutionary caveman roots. I mean *that* excuse is *so* two million years ago! However, it *is* one of three perfectly valid reasons to explain our propensity to roam.

Firstly, as males, our instinct is to spread our genes around as much as possible. Even as far as away as Costessey. This is how humans has flourished, indeed over-flourished, since our earliest beginnings. We all know that if women oversaw initiating procreation, then the human population wouldn't be much bigger than Great Plumstead.

Back in the day, and we're talking pre-Chris Hughton here, man needed to sow his seed as

BY ROGER MCCARTNEY 51

much as possible to ensure the survival and advancement of humanity. This means that the need to procreate with more than one partner, still resides deep down in our psyche – and it doesn't go away, even if we go and lie down in a darkened room. Unfortunately, we are hard-wired to have an eye for the next new partner, even when we are perfectly content with our current one.

Secondly, it doesn't take a lot to make us feel inadequate and that's exactly how we feel when we haven't had enough partners in life. This feeling of sexual inadequacy is nature's way of telling us to sleep about more. Inside every man - even those with geeky-façade - there is a serial womaniser struggling to get out. This womaniser is itching to be let out and once free, will proceed to cruise about Queen Street and pull women in Revolutions, much as in the time-honoured fashion.

Finally, there is the thrill of the chase. The need to clinch the deal goes with the

testosterone filled territory. We are like salesmen, who don't feel they can rest until they've got another signature on the dotted line. Remember Norwich men are very much chase-orientated, and the thrill derived from it. This drives us on to push up the numbers and hit our self-appointed targets.

Even with these pre-conditions working against us, Norwich men can and will stay faithful - unless a certain final fatal condition occurs – that of opportunity. Without it we are nothing. For it is written in our chromosomal make-up that men cannot resist a sexual opportunity. Even if you are the offspring of Mother Teresa, if it is there on a plate for you, you are going to be sorely tempted.

It is not just Norwich men that are love-rats either – it's just that we get all the headlines in *Eastern Daily Press*. Some of my best women friends have been love-ratesses. And worse still, some have been my partners.

BY ROGER MCCARTNEY 53

The problem with evolutionary heredity is that it takes so darn long to shake it out of our system, so don't expect any change in man's inclination to be love-rats for the next million years or so. But after that, **don't worry, we may settle down!**

Man   Secret   #11:

Norwich Men Don't do Plastic

Football is not a matter of life or death in Norwich. It is more important than that. And so is cleavage. Maybe not quite as important getting a new Narrrich top each year but it still rates highly on the must-have scale. Or, I should say, the must-view scale. And as you can tell from the fact that we are on permanent ogling standby, we are obsessed by cleavage, isn't it?

Cleavage is important because it sends an inaudible message to a man saying 'I am Woman and just as women like to accessorise, so do we Narrrwich men. I'm buzzing, for example, when I accessorise with a pretty woman, or even one

BY ROGER MCCARTNEY 55

just with the bare minimum – a pulse - on my arm.

My priorities changed, as I got older. When I was a young'un, I longed for a woman with a magnificent chest. Now I am older - I long for a woman with a personality - as well as a magnificent chest, I do. A girlfriend once said to us that I never noticed her bust, which I thought was a trifle unfair, as that was the main thing I *had* noticed. There would have been hell on if I had not noticed, I can tell you.

So, with that in mind, you might think if you asked a man if he liked implants it would be like asking a child if he wanted an extra bag of sweets. The answer would logically be in the 'corse ba! True enough, Canary men do like an enormous surgically enhanced bosom, but our fascination is in a sort of freakish sideshow type of way.

BY ROGER MCCARTNEY 56

It's a little-known fact, other than in man-cliques, that yellows man will always prefer natural to the surgically improved counterparts. There is something infinitely false and unnatural about implants. Or am I missing the point?

Enhancement of the bosom is fine but wanting to attain Katie Price proportions, well that's just scary. I would be afraid, very afraid if I found myself within the same room as that lass and her bosom. For a start, I wouldn't know where to look - as her bust will have taken up the entire available panorama. I mean is there any real need to have a bosom that big? I believe that she and her breasts really are intent on world domination. And if this is the case, I say, "You go gel!"

If Jordan *were* my woman, in some sort of parallel universe, her chest would obviously give me an inferiority complex. Trust me to look at the negatives. And, being a Norwich man, I don't do inferiority!

BY ROGER MCCARTNEY 57

MEN ARE FROM MARS
I'M FROM
NORWICH

It is not knowledge that is power in the male/female dynamic - it is cleavage. A woman armed with impressive breasts can cause us to act proper mental. If I am not careful, I will soon be doing even madder things such as gleefully picking up the tab for a takeaway Kebab.

As one of the thousands of Norwich men, masquerading as a Baywatch fan each on Saturday teatime, I can vouch that implants can have a certain surface appeal. Pamela's still dining out on her assets even now, or more recently, falling down paralytic on them.

Contrary to female opinion, when I see a woman with implants, my tongue does not roll out like an elasticised red carpet. The official Norwich perspective is this: Cleavage does not have to be as big as Norwich Cathedral to be desirable. Small is also good. And have I mentioned how underrated middle-sized is?

BY ROGER MCCARTNEY 58

MEN ARE FROM MARS
I'M FROM
NORWICH

From our point of view, there is no right or wrong with chests. **It's all good, bor.**

BY ROGER MCCARTNEY 59

<u>Man Secret #12:</u> Why Does Norwich Man Always Have to Make the First Move?

I'm not being funny, but when it comes to courtship, why is it, here on the old Wensum, that it is always the man that has to make the first move? If he doesn't, he may as well de-evolve into a single cell organism, able to replicate with himself. For that is all the attention he will get from the opposite sex.

Now that I am firmly back in the dating arena, once again I am cast as the cheetah stalking the gazelle. Proper predator me. As I leave my phone number on the car of the pretty woman in the Chapelfield shopping centre car park, I have been admiring for the last few weeks, I feel as though I am the Cheetah. The only difference in

BY ROGER MCCARTNEY 60

this scenario to the African bush is that this cheetah wants to take Miss Gazelle out for a kebab – not for her to be the kebab filling!

But just for once like, I would like to have a day off from doing predatory. Just for once, I would like to have a go at the gazelle role. Eeee, it would be nice to be on the receiving end of a pursuit for a change or what?

I learnt the 'faint heart never won fair lady lesson early in life. But ignoring lady altogether? This is not a successful tactic for the lone male to follow. You might as well sign your own single warrant.

It must be decreed somewhere in the Magna Carta that it is a woman's human right to have males-a-plenty chasing her. The last lass that came after me was when I was eight years old at Magdalen Gates Primary. She had sweet ponytails and used to pursue me round in an innocent game of playground kiss-chase.

BY ROGER MCCARTNEY 61

Naturally, I was so adept, not to mention fast at running, that I was never caught. As the game preceded my learning to kiss by about five years - thank goodness I escaped! Soon after, the roles reversed and it became the chasee's turn to become chaser and has been ever since.

Only Norwich men that have an uncanny resemblance to Messrs Pitt, Law or Clooney, don't have to sing so hard for their romantic suppers, and generally can expect to scoop up the phone numbers, without effort.

Women expect to be courted, simple as, but sometimes, I would prefer to live in a parallel universe – where the women chase us. Then I could flutter my eyelashes and reject advances with the tried and trusted line "No thanks, I'm washing my hair tonight"

Norwich men also must attain the necessary balance with our predatory tactics. Come on too strong or too fast and you might scare the

BY ROGER MCCARTNEY 62

bejesus out of her. Too laid back and you will have to go and join the back of the queue and wait until your turn comes around again.

One of life's burning questions is why is the aesthetically challenged man going out with the rather more aesthetically blessed woman. It is because he asked. He drew in his belly, pumped himself up and asked. That's a rummun. And she said yes, because she didn't have anything better to do this side of the next ice age. All women have downtime in their schedules when no Norwich men are asking. This is when a geek masquerading as Mr Nice Guy can get through. I know - I have got through several geek-force fields during my time on this planet.

If I'd known at the outset it was going to be so difficult to catch a woman, I would have let the pony-tailed one catch *us* a few more times by here, is it? Maybe I would be a better kisser as well.

BY ROGER MCCARTNEY 63

MEN ARE FROM MARS
I'M FROM
NORWICH

So, come on women: spice it up a bit, know what I mean? **Why don't you chase us for a change!**

BY ROGER MCCARTNEY 64

Man Secret #13:

Norwich Men Fall in Love More Often Than Kerry Katona.

The first week "I love you bor" was said to me once. So, after picking myself up off the floor and not wishing to appear rude; I said it right back. After exchanging the mutual love-vow with haste, we then spent the next few years unravelling the commitment, at leisure.

Such an early pledge remains a predominantly Norwich male gambit. It is one of our characteristics, when we go all starry-eyed over a new starlet in our lives; we are unable to hold back. We are in love with falling in love. But, at what point is it safe to first tell a woman of

BY ROGER MCCARTNEY 65

your love without scaring the bejesus out of her?

The need to clinch the deal goes with the testosterone filled territory. We are like car salesmen, who don't feel they can rest until they've got another signature on the dotted line. Remember Norwich men are very much chase-orientated us like and the thrill derived from it. Did you not see us last year in the Championship? We were desperate to get out of it.

In the first few days of a burgeoning relationship, there comes a point when it is necessary for the man to clinch the deal. In olden days, we would just club you over the head and point to the nearest cave. Now, because we are a little bit more sophisticated, we may use a phone to text it, but the message remains the same: we like you and we want you to move into our cave. Or more likely, can we move into your clean, tidy cave please?

BY ROGER MCCARTNEY 66

MEN ARE FROM MARS
I'M FROM
NORWICH

Pitch this message too soon and the relationship may self-destruct. A premature utterance of 'I love you gel' will cause a woman to run for the hills just as surely as Gazza turning up in Norwich for a meet and greet.

I once knew a woman; she was not English as she spoke it far too well. Our first kiss had gone smoothly, and her bruised toe was recovering nicely from where I had stood on it. Love-bites had been exchanged and horizontal relations were on the horizon. The schoolboy error was not, in the note thanking her for a lovely evening - it was in the added PS - that I was falling in love with her.

Naturally, Miss Non-Reciprocal gozzed us out quicker than an undercooked kebab. When I rang to enquire, a few days later, why she had moved back to Cringleford finally got the answer. "It's because you said you love me".

BY ROGER MCCARTNEY 67

Oh, I see! That explains it. Maybe the government can get illegal immigrants to go back home by telling them that **I** have fallen in love with them?

"You never tell a woman you love her, never!" exclaimed my ol mate. Whilst, I noted his comments, I couldn't help noticing too, the lack of female companionship. I also wondered about the colour of the sky in his world. But I noted he did indeed have Sky in his world, so I vowed to be round next Sunday to watch it!

Obviously, my newly ensconced Cringleford-based ex-lover, thought I was some sort of plank who gets his kicks from falling hopelessly for women after three dates. Well, she was about as spot on as she could get - for I *am* that plank.

I had acted like a young'un in the game of love – which, being only 42 at the time was

BY ROGER MCCARTNEY 68

understandable. I was only trying to bring her closer, not make her flee the City altogether.

We do delude ourselves though. No matter how much I jolly well force myself - I can't fall in love with someone I met just two days ago. It's that old devil called lust – masquerading as love again bor.

Sometimes it is good to get 'I love you' out during the first week, meaningless or not. If she walks, then so be it – Cringleford is very nice. In fact, to weed out the timewasters, I'm thinking of starting my next relationship with asking **"Hello, I love you! Won't you tell me your name."** Or was that the Doors?

BY ROGER MCCARTNEY 69

Man Secret #14:
Norwich Men Don't Do Home Improvement.

It's that time of year again – when wallpaper sample books appear, and Norwich blokes take cover behind the sofa that we will soon be asked to re-position. No, it is not a new series of *Doctor Who* – but time to re-decorate.

The reason for the process is simple. Most couples desire the biggest and best property they can afford. Ideally, they want a palatial residence, but cannot always get one because of restrictions in affluence. It is therefore necessary to achieve the palatial effect in their modest home – by decorating the hell out of it.

Each gender's strengths will be played to in the decoration process. Female brain will be used to

BY ROGER MCCARTNEY 70

MEN ARE FROM MARS
I'M FROM
NORWICH

conceptualise, whilst male brawn will be utilised during implementation. No doubt, Norwich men are naturals at DIY. The fashioning of items out of wood, stone and iron appeals directly to our inner caveman, and our Norwich roots. But decorating – should be left to the professionals or failing that - women.

Sure, Norwich men can point a drill at the wall and move seemingly insurmountable pieces of furniture, as efficiently as Samson can, but women have ownership of the embellishment skills.

The Female of the species is more deadly than the male – at the arranging of the sequinned cushions, and the placing of the yin/yang ornaments, picked up from Norwich market. Women are, by instinct, nest makers and therefore by extension – nest decorators. It is an innate thing.

BY ROGER MCCARTNEY 71

Cynon-side men, in their chromosomal make-up, have deficiencies in certain genes that inhibit their decorating ability - particularly the taste gene. They can recognise colours but are unable to co-ordinate them. They are also deficient in the try-to-look-interested gene. Women, however, have both genes in abundance.

Norwich men do not attempt this at home! Put the lava lamp down and move away from the net curtains!

Furnishing is a subject that I have always filed in the mental 'don't-care-about' drawer. I thought *décor* was a type of decaffeinated coffee. And why scatter cushions? Why not just place them sensibly?

In most couples, women are allowed *carte blanche* to furnish. For Health & Safety purposes, it is sensible for a man to interfere or question her about her decorating decisions, only if he is wearing a hard hat. Furthermore,

BY ROGER MCCARTNEY 72

MEN ARE FROM MARS
I'M FROM
NORWICH

failure to complete tasks assigned to him, satisfactorily, may call his masculinity into question.

NR1 men are also shackled by the fact that they lied early in the relationship about their interest in home improvement. Big mistake - the refurbishment genie is out of the bottle and you must now feed the voracious appetite that women have for consistently transforming the dwelling space.

Decorating is like restoring Norwich Cathedral: once you finish, you need to start all over. My view is that it is far better not to start decorating in the first place and live in abject squalor.

She may seduce you into watching home improvement TV programs, in the hope that you will be inspired. You may well feel inspired - to flee. The will to live will also slowly drain from

BY ROGER MCCARTNEY 73

your body new schedule of tasks is assigned to you.

A good way to make up for the lack of new furniture coming in is to get more creative with existing furniture, by re-arranging the layout. Careful, Norwich men, that it is not *you* that is spoiling the ambience of the place - otherwise *you* might be re-positioned - outside the front door. Her ultimate interior plan may be that '*Chez Nous*', **should become simply, '*Chez Moi*'.**

BY ROGER MCCARTNEY 74

MEN ARE FROM MARS
I'M FROM
NORWICH

Man Secret #15:

Norwich Man is God's Gift to Romance (At The Start)

You must agree that at the start of a relationship, Norwich men are god's gift to romance. We will organise a kebab, buy some flowers from the Co-op on Earlham Road, and trawl round the gift stalls on the market for matching his and her key rings. Just as any bog-standard lovesick fool would. Whilst I am mooching around, she will do what she does best – transform into the visual equivalent of a million dollars by clarting herself right up proper like.

At the beginning, it's all about the chase. This is why I am romantic. I have to be. Faint heart never won fair lady. If I'm not romantic, then

BY ROGER MCCARTNEY 75

MEN ARE FROM MARS
I'M FROM
NORWICH

it's 666333. Hello, is that ABC Taxis**? Taxi for McCartney please!** You're going home alone, fair lady-less, bor.

I will initiate the courtship moves, when we slow dance, and she will initiate the moving away moves. The first kiss will usually also emanate from the male side. And the first slap from the female side, if the timing is not right.

Evolution has given Norwich men the role of pursuers and Norwich women traditionally have the role of pursuees. I wish it wasn't the case as I wouldn't mind being pursued for a change, but it's not going to happen. Not unless I join a boyband. And that may be unrealistic; bearing in mind I am no longer a boy.

It is only when the chase is over, and the prize secured that we become romantic dullards. It's like DIY. All the skills are there but the toolbox doesn't come out very often. We will then only rise to the romantic occasion on Valentine's Day. It is not, as you might suspect that our ardour

BY ROGER MCCARTNEY 76

begins to wane. It is more because our true reserved nature begins to win the battle for internal control.

When it comes to being romantic, we are Jeckyl and Hide lovers. We are capable of great love and romance such as on Valentine's Day. Then there is the other side of us where we have been told for centuries to keep a stiff upper lip whilst conquering the globe. This is the everyday partner you see before you today, aka romantic dullard.

It's not that we fall out of love. It's that we feel a fool, for showing love. Even when we were initiating the chase and making all the romantic overtures at the start, we didn't feel right. Sure, we were good at it, but it didn't feel right. We Norwich men are naturally reserved. We haven't shaken the Victorian out of us yet. Give us a chance. It's only been a hundred or so years.

BY ROGER MCCARTNEY 77

MEN ARE FROM MARS
I'M FROM
NORWICH

You see inside every bloke there is a swashbuckling, falling-from-a-top-of-The-Forum-to-deliver-chocolates-type-of-guy. Conversely, inside Mr Start-of-Romance there is boring block of stone, waiting to break out and slump down in front of Sky TV. This version of male will breeze past the flowers stall at Tesco without giving it a moment's thought.

How do you keep the romance alive? In my experience, women are also Jekyll and Hide lovers, not so much romantically, but sexually. Mrs Hide may also tend to hijack the female persona once the first flush is gone.

If you can keep your sexual Dr Jekyll alive i.e. by wearing erotic pyjamas or something along those lines, then he is more likely to keep his romantic Dr Jekyll to the fore, **and get down to the Co-op in Earlham Road to buy you flowers the next day.**

BY ROGER MCCARTNEY 78

Man Secret #16: Are Norwich Men Up for It? And I Don't Mean the Cup?

It is a question that has haunted mankind since the dawn of time. "Why are we here?" Simple: we are here to push on from last season. We all know that. But this question pales into insignificance when compared to "should I sleep with someone on a first date"?"

Now, as Narrrwich men, we have the morality code of the lesser-spotted orang-utan. Norwich women also have a morality code – that of the greater-spotted orang-utan. You see, it's several notches higher. They have the high ground.

If you are used to using a high-morality blocker of say, factor ten, then you are going to block

BY ROGER MCCARTNEY 79

out the attraction rays from the opposite sex altogether. If you want an all over appeal, keep your morality blocker low, and then some sex will creep through.

But why would you possibly want to sleep with someone on a first date? Three things: chemistry, opportunity and alcohol. It is like the ingredients for fire. Any one ingredient on its own = a damp squib. But put them all together and in the right quantities and you're going to get burnt baby!

What to look for: Norwich men – look for someone in the Jennifer Anniston mode, preferably in a Norwich replica shirt. Don't worry if she doesn't look like the goddess that is Jennifer Anniston to start with; just have a few beers. She will slowly start to resemble the actress we all desire, the more beers you have. Women – if he looks anything remotely like David de Gea – then he's a keeper!

BY ROGER MCCARTNEY 80

Scientists have come up with a formula to explain the scientific rationale of the chances of sleeping with someone, on the initial meeting. Why? Because it's fashionable.

(Attraction + Chemistry + Opportunity + Alcohol) > Morality of participants = Sex.

If the sum of the first four mood enhancers is greater than the combined morality inhibitors of the two participants, then sex will occur. You can't argue with science.

Whether he will call you the next day or not is the next in the series of life's burning questions. Perhaps we need another formula, the *Bastard Equation*, to work out if he's likely to call.

If the sex was good, he'll call. If the sex was out of this world, he'll Facebook you within five minutes. In fact, some of his friends might even Facebook you as well.

BY ROGER MCCARTNEY 81

MEN ARE FROM MARS
I'M FROM
NORWICH

Non-returning of calls is not exclusive behaviour of the male sex, either. Many a lad rings a girl the next day only to find he has been given Radio 1's flirt divert number and his soppy message, professing un-dying love, is liable to be read out live to six million people.

Of course, each person has his or her own individual score on the moral-ometer. Zero = morals of alley cat. Ten = routine use of chastity belt. My own score is round about the one/two mark, whereas, most of my dates are around nine. Memo to self: stop arranging dates with women from the Thorpe End knitting circle.

The chances of making it to bed with someone, first night, are ridiculously low anyway.

Here's my checklist.

1) Is there any attraction shown by her towards us other than the sort of casual interest she

BY ROGER MCCARTNEY 82

would have towards the Tapir enclosure at Banham Zoo?

2) Has she bought the 'I have a PhD in nuclear physics, which I studied in between sessions at the gym' line?

3) Did she laugh when she asked you if you had a police record and you replied "Yes. Message in a Bottle"

4) You ask her back to your place and she doesn't call the Norfolk Police. I'm not in the mood for any chew like.

5) Now she's back at your place and if you can function at all after all the alcohol you have imbibed, then you're on to a winner.

6) Wait a minute, you didn't realise there was two of them. Oh well, even better.

7) You can't function. Roll over. Go to sleep.

Of course, I'll sleep with someone on a first date, me. It would be rude not to. But due to the vast quantities of alcohol consumed, sleep is all I will do! And I **will** phone her the next day, for I fall in love more often than Kerry Katona,

BY ROGER MCCARTNEY 83

me like. In fact, sometimes I fall in love with Kerry Katona. But that's another story.

So, expect to hear me on radio 1, any day now.

MEN ARE FROM MARS
I'M FROM
NORWICH

Man Secret #17: Canary Men Worry About Being Fat, Just as Much as Norwich Women.

My stomach's plans for world domination must be thwarted. Norwich Cathedral no longer dominates the skyline. My stomach does. Doing nothing is not an option. Besides, doing nothing is so last week. It was precisely doing nothing that allowed the paunch to grab a belly-hold.

Women **do not** have ownership of the weight control problem. Fat transcends the gender boundaries and men suffer the angst of weight-watching too. For women, it traditionally affects the hips whereas in my case it is more tummy centric. My waistline is like the Larkman on a Saturday night – it needs to be continually policed.

BY ROGER MCCARTNEY 85

I look back with rose-tinted fondness to the days when Delia Smith was just a dinner lady and I didn't have to wrestle a spare tyre into my trousers each morning. The problem first arrived when I was in my middle-twenties. I woke up one day, and there the beer-belly was, like Jeremy Corbyn – in it for the long haul. Other companions come and go, but it seems that me and my belly is one relationship that really *is* for life.

Sometimes I feel like letting the potbelly win the battle. I feel like saying to it: "OK. You can have me house, me Norwich replica shirt, whatever – just leave us alone like."

Sure, I will slim down when there is an important project, for which it is essential to get in shape. Currently, I am engaged in the 'trying-not-to-morph-into-Johnny-Vegas' project. Also, whenever my flab is beginning to hamper the chances of procreation, then it is time for action.

BY ROGER MCCARTNEY 86

So, why is the belly an initiator of such anxiety amongst us canary men? It is simply because it is unattractive to the opposite sex. If it wasn't – I'd have two, please! Gerrus one of them kebabs for me and one for my best mate, the belly, please.

If my figure repulses *me* – and I'm a fan of me - then what chance it will appeal to anyone with the prized double x chromosomes? I wish to attract as many women as possible; not just those that are Tele tubby-tolerant.

You know that saying "the past is a place I don't want to live, but it's worth visiting now and then"? well I wouldn't mind living there permanently, thank you very much, is it? I was skinny then, back in the day, I was. I spent the first half of my life as a skinny stick insect. It was bootiful. If girls approached at the beach, it was to kick sand in my face. I was as happy as the proverbial.

BY ROGER MCCARTNEY 87

Now if women approach, it is just to spend time in the shade that my bulk provides. I did experience a brief window of appearance-acceptability in my middle twenties – a couple of distress-free months during the transition from skinny to fat - and then it was on with the headlong slide into obesity.

Funny how priorities change! When asked at school, what I wanted to be, who could have foretold that a more realistic lifegoal, rather than be centre forward for Norwich Town, would be to walk to the local Co-op in Earlham Road, without getting out of breath. How dare they build in a mechanism such as getting fat, to stop us gorging our faces off?

I am in self-imposed exile from Patisserie Valley in the Town centre as the selection of cream cakes is simply too alluring. By 2000, my life had spiralled out of control and I was on 200 grams of chocolate a day. I wasn't a dealer – it was for personal use only.

BY ROGER MCCARTNEY 88

So, I knocked all that on the head. Apart from the customary seven pints a night, I have retained only the one other 'pig out' behaviour – the Sunday roast. I devour it with haste, and then I can spend the whole of the following week repenting at leisure.

Another tactic I utilise is the wearing of extra-large shirts. I figure that no one will realise I'm overweight if I disguise myself as a marquee.

I could try the heartbreak diet. Again. The only thing is, I'm out of the loop - so I would need to fall in love; behave badly for three years; get dumped; before the diet could kick in.

But don't worry. I'm pleased to announce the onslaught of plumpness is under control. **My waist is diminishing and my moobs are down to an attractive C cup.**

BY ROGER MCCARTNEY 89

Man Secret #18:
Norwich Men are Commitaphobe.

Have you ever had one of those moments? When you walk in a room like a right plank and lose the plot as to why you're by there?

I lose the bigger picture plot sometimes. I know there is something I've forgotten to do. Then I remember – "Oh, yes. Get married and have mini-Narrrwich citizens.

It dawned on me recently that the purpose of life is _not_ to have a good time. It is to procreate and pass on those fiddly little things, genes.

It was last week, as my forty-second birthday bore down on me, that the penny finally dropped. Duh. Hello! Earth calling Roger! In the

BY ROGER MCCARTNEY 90

past, birthdays resulted in boozy celebrations up the Eagle on the Newmarket Road. Now, I am more likely to embark on a session of binge thinking, about where I went wrong in life. How did Mr Eligible morph into Johnny no-kids?

I never wanted junior Norwich-residents – till now. Now that my fathering equipment is a bit battered and probably doesn't work anymore. I've always had a *chaplinesque* approach to fatherhood and had back-burnered the whole idea until later in life.

Now I feel like shouting to the world, "Give me a kid. Oh, and a woman. And see what you can do about North Korea, will you?" I would love to see a little Roger or Rogella running about.

For years I shunned commitment. Now I embrace it. I welcome it. I feel like saying "come in, commitment, and sit in my favourite chair by the fire and watch *Match of the Day*

BY ROGER MCCARTNEY 91

with me. And bring all your child rearing possibilities with you!"

Failure to commit is not always voluntary. A lot of it is 'wrong place, wrong time' syndrome. I cannot even blame it on my own broken-home childhood. We get the point. It was grim. Move on.

I never found *The One*. It is difficult enough to find *one* at all, let alone *one* with special qualities that would necessitate calling her *The One*.

I thought I had found *The One*. And I had: *The One* that lived around the corner from me in George Borrow Road. She spoke very highly of me. She looked like the blonde one in Abba and had roughly the same impact on me as the blonde one in Abba had on the rest of the world. She was a cathedral in my life: a massive monument and somewhere to go and worship. It was not so much a match made in heaven as a

BY ROGER MCCARTNEY 92

match made in the Beehive. Our souls would be interlocked forever. And they were too. Well, for ten months of it. I was happy as. Unfortunately, she wasn't. I wasn't *The One* for her, but some pasty-faced get from Brundall was. He was soft as shite and twice as smelly.

Further auditions for *Wife Idol* were held but all roads leading to marriage turned out to be cul-de-sacs; where you have to do one of those awkward U turns to get out. You go all the way down by there for naff all is it?

That put the mockers on that. I was like Irvine in the window, I just couldn't clinch the deal. I was far too immature – I had only just learnt to tie my shoelaces - whilst under the influence – and so I partied like it was 1999.

1999 came. Party over. Ace Cabs for McCartney. All the guests had gone home or got married. Just as I was envisaging a *Last of the Summer*

BY ROGER MCCARTNEY 93

MEN ARE FROM MARS
I'M FROM
NORWICH

Wine future with my two mates – they got married. No, not to each other, fool!

I was always the best man and never the groom. One day, Forty came up and gave me a coupla taps on the shoulder. I politely requested 'can I not cadge another twenty years of prime time' but Forty replied 'yaravinalaffarnya!'

So, you see the City Hall clock tower is ticking. Sitting on the shelf is no longer an option. I am still looking for *The One*. The nearest I've got so far to *The One* is watching *The One Show*. But there is still time. Time is what we *do* have. A willing baby-machine is what we *don't* have. But I'm working on it. I went into *Babies R Us* and asked for a baby the other day. They looked at me as if I was from Norwich.

So, what are the chances of mother turning into grandmother any time soon? **As a great magician – not from Narrrwich, I hasten to add - used to say, "Not a Lot!"**

BY ROGER MCCARTNEY 94

MEN ARE FROM MARS
I'M FROM
NORWICH

Hope you enjoyed the book folks.

BY ROGER MCCARTNEY 95

Printed in Great Britain
by Amazon